Financial Freedom for All

Financial Independence, Unlimited Wealth, Smart Investing, Saving

Brock Minton

Table of Contents

Introduction

If you're tired of living paycheck to paycheck, and if you're sick of watching your account balance dwindle to nothing by the end of the month, it's time to consider changing your spending habits and working on acquiring financial freedom. When most people hear the words *financial freedom,* they either picture the elite—the one percent, living it up in their mansions, owning yachts, and going on fancy vacations—or they picture people who are self-employed and run their own businesses. Achieving financial freedom may come off as a pipe dream for many of us, who work 9–5 jobs and struggle to have any savings at the end of the month.

However, that is simply not true. Attaining true financial freedom can be a possibility for you, no matter what income bracket you belong to. You could be a successful business owner or work a 9–5 job in an office, or even work behind a register at a supermarket. No matter your profession, you can still be financially independent and save money—if only you can figure out how.

This is where this book can help. We will tell you everything you need to know about managing your money smartly, how to budget, how to save, how to invest, and how to spend money. It is a complete guide on money management, with financial independence being the ultimate goal.

Think about it this way; how many times have you sighed wistfully at the end of the month, looking at something you wanted to buy online but simply did not have the funds? How many sleepless nights have you had to bear, knowing that your paycheck is about to run out and not knowing how you will manage until your next payday? How many times have you found yourself wishing that you had some savings so you could maybe travel, or buy property, or have more financial security for your children?

The truth that nobody wants you to know is that you can have all of this! You can have everything you want; all you need to know is how to get it. The reality is that most of us are clueless when it comes to managing money. It's not a class that we ever had to take at school, and there are very few of us whose parents sat us down and gave us a complete rundown on how to manage money. There are many adults, who to this day, get confused when they go to the bank, who have no idea how to budget, and who spend money as soon as they get some as if there is no tomorrow. This has created a generation of frivolous spenders. Even people who think they are conscientious with money end up getting befuddled at the end of the month when their bank account says otherwise.

It's never too late to change. With the help of this book, you can not only learn how to manage your money better, but you will learn how to be more organized in your spending and make smart fiscal decisions. You will learn how to spend money according to your income and how not to spend beyond your means. Having money is crucial to surviving in this world; you need to be comfortable and live your life independently without being a burden on your relatives or the government. Being rich is not magic; the richest people in the world are those who can manage their money well.

No matter how much money you earn—you could earn millions of dollars—there may come a day when the money runs out if you do not know how to manage it well. Granted, most of us do not make millions of dollars, but whatever money you do make, this book will teach you how you can manage it. We'll cover how you can accumulate substantial savings, how to supplement your income and grow your wealth, and how you can save not only for your benefit but for the benefit of your family, your children, and their grandchildren. This book will help you learn to build your financial legacy, and it's all explained in a simple, straightforward manner that anybody can implement!

Who Should Read This Book?

To be honest, this book is aimed at anyone who is looking to solidify their financial freedom and is hoping to be financially independent and free in the near future. It is never too late to start down the road; however, it is certainly worth noting that the sooner you start, the easier things will become.

In this book, I have covered some of the most secure ways of earning, investing, and savings that the world continues to use. Yes, it takes time, which is why you will not come across anything that allows you to become a millionaire overnight. For anyone who claims that they know of ways that can make you rich overnight, or in a ridiculously short span of time, just walk away. Anything that sounds too good to be true is probably just that.

You can be a fresh graduate, a mid-aged professional, a stay-at-home parent, or a teacher, and you can still use the ideas highlighted within this book as inspiration to work towards your financial freedom. Financial freedom is everyone's birthright, but only a few are willing to do what it takes to achieve it. Most people go throughout their lives trying to find something that will work for them. I am here to ensure that you do not have to continue searching for such methods, most of which may not work out for you. In this book, I will only discuss aspects and matters that will provide you with high chances of success and healthy returns.

With consistency, a bit of knowledge, and the right moves, you should be able to create a sustainable passive income and a good savings account, all of which will help you accelerate your journey to attain financial freedom. You do not need to worry about having relevant knowledge or experience, as I will teach you all that you should know.

I will also ensure not to use difficult or intimidating terminologies unnecessarily as that may negate the point of the book, which is to teach everyone how to achieve financial freedom. Where necessary, I will use these terms and explain these as we proceed further.

A Word of Caution

With that said, I would like to clarify that any investment idea that you come across in this book is based on research, personal experiences, and other documented data. They may or may not work for everyone, which is why it is best to find out more about whatever it is that you are willing to invest in beforehand. This is particularly important for foreign exchange (forex) trading, as most of the websites and platforms highlight how over 80% of the traders end up losing money. Where there is money, there is bound to be some risk. However, the higher the risks, the higher the rewards. Ideally, you should aim to invest a sum of money that you are okay to lose in the worst-case scenario. Do not put every cent into something that is volatile or insecure in nature. It is recommended that you invest your money in a variety of options, just to ensure that you are still making profits if one fails.

Chapter 1: How to Set Your Financial Goals

Many of us get discouraged and disheartened with our finances in life, especially when we seem to be making endless payments without having anything to show for it. Have you ever felt like you're shoveling a ton of money into paying off debt without making a dent in the final amount you owe? And even after working like a dog for years, is a crappy car and a shoebox apartment all you have to show for it? Do you make a budget at the beginning of the month but still, things never end up as planned?

Don't worry; we've all been there. What you need to realize is that you need to put a plan behind your finances. If you don't, then money will simply slip through your fingers without you even realizing where it went. If you don't aim at anything, you'll end up hitting everything. The point is, if you want to manage your money, instead of letting your money manage you, you need to set some financial goals in place.

What Are Financial Goals?

A financial goal is a plan that you set for your money. Any payments that you have to make and any expenditures that you have lined up constitute financial goals. If you're saving up to buy a car or a house, that is a financial goal. If you're saving money for a vacation or a cosmetic procedure, that counts as a financial goal. You could also be working at paying off debt or building an emergency fund; all of these constitute financial goals.

Having financial goals can help keep your spending habits in check.

Financial goals can be short-term, mid-term, and long-term. Establishing these goals is a vital step in moving towards becoming financially secure. If you don't have any specific financial goals, you end up spending way more money than you realize or you should. Then, usually, we'd end up falling short on bills or end up taking money out of our savings. Without financial goals, it's easy to get stuck in a crazy cycle of credit card debt without ever having enough cash to get good insurance or getting debtors off your back, leaving you extremely financially vulnerable and ill-equipped to handle life's risks.

Why Is Having Financial Goals Important?

If you have set financial goals, it will change your approach towards your money. You will experience a paradigm shift, noticing how every decision you make has an impact on your financial status. If you don't have any financial goals, it's very easy to make frivolous purchases. You would buy that cup of artisan coffee on your way to work, even though you could perfectly make coffee at home. It's easy, it's delicious, and it's only a few extra bucks. However, those few extra bucks add up, sometimes as much as 25–30 dollars per week. You could do a lot with that money.

For example, if you put a hundred dollars into an investment account each month for five years, your coffee fund would end up growing into more than $7,000 due to compounding interest! That could pay off a semester in college for your kids—which you're now paying your local coffee shop for fancy coffee.

If you invest $100 for 15 years instead, you could grow your coffee savings to almost $45,000 to $50,000. I'm sure there's a lot you can do with fifty thousand dollars at any time in your life! More time equals more money; saving the same hundred bucks for 30 years could get you more than $280,000. So, the choice should be easy to make. A fancy coffee every day or $280,000 in your savings account later on? It should be a no-brainer.

You have to sacrifice to be financially secure, and those sacrifices can help you attain your financial goals. The way you interact with your money in the present will determine how much of it you have in the future.

How to Set Financial Goals: A Step-by-Step Guide

Now that you know why it is so important to set financial goals, we can work on establishing how you can set financial goals. It's not a difficult process once you know where to begin. Setting the goals is the easy part; following through on the implementation of these goals is where the hard work begins.

So how can you set financial goals for yourself?

Step One: Figure Out What Matters to You

Your goals should be a reflection of your needs and wants. You need to carefully consider not only what you want to do but why you want to do it. If you understand the reason behind your goals, it will help give perspective about achieving them and motivate you along the way.

Deliberate and figure out what matters to you. It could range from practical and substantial to completely whimsical and out of the ordinary, but if it's important to you and relevant to your goals, you should make it a part of your financial goals. First, put everything on the table, then evaluate your goals and earnings and the time it would take to save up. Decide what expenses should take priority over others and which nuisance expenses you should get rid of first. For example, pay off your nuisance credit card debt so you can start saving towards an emergency fund or a wedding.

Step Two: Examine Your Situation

It might be that you discover that you have a lot of goals and no idea where to begin. It could also be that you don't have any specific goals in mind, which is fine. You just need to take a good, hard look at where you currently stand, so you set off in the right direction, regardless of whether you have long-term or short-term ambitions.

The first thing you need to do is evaluate your income, where you stand on taxes, how much you can allocate for a budget, and what your net worth is. Once you have a better understanding of these four things, you will have an easier time setting your goals and prioritizing them accordingly.

Be specific when you're setting your goals. Your goal shouldn't sound like "I want to have more savings this year." That is very vague and ambiguous. Your goals should be very specific. For example, say, "I will save $300 every month." A set amount gives you an easier goal to work towards.

Here are a few examples of good financial goals:

Building an Emergency Fund

Emergency expenses such as medical bills tend to spring up out of nowhere and take us unaware. For precisely such a situation, an emergency reserve could be a security blanket during times where we experience severe financial shock, such as a big medical bill, a fine, or if you lose your job. A good sum for an emergency fund should be enough to cover at least three to six months' worth of expenses, and you should at least have five hundred dollars tucked away at all times.

Save for Retirement

You might be young and in the workforce now, but you won't be young forever. It is crucial to start saving for your retirement so you won't be left out in the cold once you're too old to earn a living. Financial experts recommend saving 15% of your gross income annually for your retirement. If your employer offers a retirement plan (a 401(k) in America and there are versions of that in almost every country), take advantage of that plan as it's free money.

Pay off Debt

Make paying off toxic, high interest, nuisance debt first, such as credit card bills. Then you can pay off lower interest debt like student loans.

Step Three: Be Smart

Smart is an acronym that helps you settle your financial goals. When you consider all the necessary components of a plan, you need to consider the path you will take to reach that goal, not just the goal itself. Whenever you're setting a goal, you have to make sure it's smart. Smart stands for specific, measurable, achievable, realistic, time-bound.

Suppose your goal is saving up for a holiday abroad. You need to iron out all the details before you purchase the ticket; you need to select your destination, the time of your travel, how many days you need off from work, and what the overall cost of the trip will be. Analyze whether this is an attainable goal; it should be practical most of all, considering your income, your savings, and expenses. If your new financial goal seems completely fantastical and unattainable, try to alter your plans before ditching them altogether. Sometimes making cutbacks works just as well. You just have to know where to make them.

If you haven't reached your financial goal, for example, saving up for a vacation in six months, don't cancel your plans, and instead push back your deadline. In the meantime, you can open up a new savings account, one that has a higher interest rate and a sign-up bonus to fatten your savings. You can also try automating your savings to keep a better check on them.

Step Four: Write Your Goals Down

Writing down your financial goals will do wonders for accountability. After you've figured out and vetted your goals, write them down so you can keep focused on your objectives. Make sure your objectives are clear but also well-organized and attainable. You can use a spreadsheet on your computer or jot down notes in a journal or a notepad. Refer back to your list from time to time to keep abreast of your progress. When you achieve one goal, consider it an accomplishment and move on towards setting the next.

Whenever you write your goals down, you end up being more likely to achieve them. Writing your financial goals is like committing yourself. A good trick is to keep your goals in sight; make a vision board, stick them to your desk or your mirror. The more accessible your goals are, the more you will look at them and end up manifesting them as well.

Step Five: Treat Yourself!

Saving money doesn't always have to be drudgery and self-sacrifice. Some financial goals, granted, are boring, like paying off credit card debt. But they don't always have to seem like a chore. Once you accomplish your higher priority goals like paying off your debt and saving up for an emergency fund, you can start saving up for things that you've always wanted but never could afford. Make exciting goals; these could range from anything like saving up for a holiday, cosmetic surgery, buying designer or luxury items, or simply making more money! That way, you reward yourself for being so good and saving all the money for such a long time.

Don't compare your goals to other people; your financial goals are unique to you, and you will be able to accomplish them only if you're committed to them.

Chapter 2: How to Budget Your Money

A budget is crucial if you have a limited paycheck and abundant expenses. A budget is a summary of your finances that tracks your earnings and expenditures for a set period. Most people design their budgets every month.

When people hear the word *budget*, they associate it with restrictions. However, that is not always the case. A successful budget does not always need to be restrictive. You can create a budget for your spending or your household spending as well.

A budget will help you decide how much money you can expect to save. You can compare your earnings to your expenses, which would include your bills, grocery money, rent, and other miscellaneous expenditures such as shopping or eating out. You should not view your budget as something negative; having a positive approach will help you stick to it more easily. Consider your budget as a means of achieving your financial goals, and you will be more motivated to follow through and stick to it.

Purpose of a Budget

A budget is a written financial planning tool that helps you plan your savings and spending every month. You can track where your money goes and notice your spending trends and habits. Even though making a budget can seem dreary and overwhelming to some, it is very important to keep your financial situation on track.

Budgets help you keep track of your finances because they are dependent on balance. If you overspend in one area, you can scrimp on another to compensate. You'll want to save money for important purchases and a rainy day. You can also consider investing in wealth-building schemes that will help you grow your savings. Your budget will ultimately show you how much you earn, how much you save, and where you spend all your money every month.

How to Set a Budget

If you want to set a budget that works and helps you live a smooth and comfortable life, you need to gain control of what you are spending at the moment. Note how much you can afford to spend and what your priorities are. You can use one of the numerous budget templates available online to set your budget and track your expenses and earnings.

The first thing you need to do when you're setting a budget is to calculate how much money you earn every month. There are different budgeting methods that you can follow, some of which will be discussed in this book later on.

One of the most efficient ways to calculate your budget is using the 50/30/20 rule. This rule helps you create a basic budgeting framework. You should allocate up to 50% of your income for your day-to-day expenses and everyday needs and 30% of your income for your wants. Learn how to differentiate between your needs and wants, and you will have a much easier time allocating your budget and setting financial goals. Make a personal commitment to save at least 20% of your earnings or use them to pay off debt. You need to pay off debt first if you hope to save any money at all.

Understand the Budgeting Process

Before you set your budget, have a checklist that helps you ascertain the budgeting process. You will need to do the following things:

- Figure out your after-tax income: Study your paycheck and determine how much money you make after taxes and other deductions. If you have any supplementary sources of income, add that to your net income and calculate the total amount of money you have to spend per month for your budget.
- Choose your budgeting plan: We will discuss ideal budget plans in detail later on.
- Track your progress: You can keep track of your spending using online budgeting and saving tools (which you can Google to find).
- Automate your savings: You should automate your financial transactions as much as possible so you can achieve your purpose without making a lot of effort. These days, you can set up your accounts to handle bills and expenses on their own without you logging into your internet banking account.
- Revise your budget when needed: Your spending habits and income will keep changing, so make sure you revise your budget accordingly.

How to Make a Budget in Six Easy Steps

Now that you understand what goes into making a budget, let's discuss precisely how you can set your budget in six simple steps.

Step One: Collect All Your Financial Paperwork

Before you start making your budget, you need to make sure all of your financial paperwork is in order to get a true picture of your earnings. Collect all of your financial statements before you begin, including but not limited to your bank statements, investment accounts, recent utility bills, pay slips, credit card bills, receipts from the previous three months, mortgage or any other loan statements, and any other documentation regarding your finances. You should have access to all the information about your earnings and your expenditures. The salient point of any budget-making process is to create a monthly average number, and you can only do this if you are fully informed about the state of your finances.

Step Two: Calculate Your Income

You need to know exactly how much money you earn per month to create an effective budget. Ask yourself, "How much am I earning this month?" If you get paid via a regular paycheck complete with automatically deducted taxes, then you can simply use your take-home pay amount for your budgeting needs. However, if you have outside sources of income such as alimony payments or child-support income or are self-employed, you need to factor in those earnings as well. Record the total amount of money you get as your overall income, which would become your monthly amount.

Do note that it's very easy to overestimate what you think you can afford if you think of your total earnings as spendable money. You should not view your entire salary as spending money—remember to account for expenses like your taxes, bills, social security, and other necessary expenditures. You should also have flexible spending account allocations whenever you're working on your budget. Your take-home salary is called your net income. You should create your budget based on your net income.

Step Three: Create a List of Your Monthly Expenses

The most efficient budgets are in the form of a list. Sit down at the beginning of every month and list out all of the expenses you know you will have to pay during one month. Your list could include the following: your mortgage and car payments, any insurance payments, your monthly groceries, and utility bills. Along with that, you should allocate spending money for entertainment and personal care (which includes medical expenses if you do not have health insurance). Also, be sure to factor in expenses like eating out, childcare if you have kids, and transportation costs (which could include both public transport and fuel for your car). Other expenses could include credit card payments, student loans, setting money aside for savings, etc.

It might seem overwhelming, but it's quite easy to stay on top of things once you're organized. You can take all your bank statements, credit card statements, and receipts from the previous three months to keep track of all that you're spending.

Step Four: Determine Fixed and Variable Expenses

Step four is more of a continuation of step three. It needs you to identify which of your expenses are fixed and which are variable for you to set your budget accordingly. So what do these terms mean?

Fixed expenses are the necessary expenses that you absolutely cannot get away with not paying. You have to pay the same amount every month, such as for your mortgage or rent, car payments, internet service, any other services such as garbage collection, and any other important payments that are the same every month. It would be a good idea to also save a fixed amount of money or determine a fixed amount to pay off debt each month. This way, you could also include debt repayment and savings as your fixed expenses, making you more accountable for payments.

Variable expenses, on the other hand, are payments that vary in amount every month, such as your grocery bill, how much you pay for gas, how much you spend on entertainment and eating out, and how much other miscellaneous shopping you do every month.

Assign a spending value to each type of expense. Start with fixed expenses and allocate money for them, then allocate money for variable expenses after figuring out how much you will spend on these expenses per month.

Most people are not sure about how much money they spend for either category. To be sure, review your credit card or bank transactions over the last couple of months to get a ballpark figure of your spending.

Step Five: Add up Your Monthly Income and Subtract Your Expenses

If you are amongst the lucky people whose income is higher than your expenses, congratulations, you're already taking a running start. The extra money you make can be allocated towards funding different areas in your budget, such as saving for retirement or paying off any debt you might have.

Those who do have a higher income than their expenses can consider adopting the 50/30/20 rule to budgeting, as we mentioned at the beginning of this chapter. If your income is much less than your expenses, it means that you are spending too much money and your spending habits need to change.

Step Six: Adjust Your Expenses

If you are in a position where you are not earning enough money to cover all your expenses, find an area in your variable expenses that you can reduce. Look over your expenses and figure out places where you can cut your spending, such as not eating out as much or sacrificing a luxury like a gym membership.

The goal should be to have an equal amount for both your income and expense columns. An equal balance is ideal, as it means that you can account for all sources of your income and budget towards paying off any specific expense or adding to your savings. If you have expenses that are far above your income or have insurmountable debt, then just cutting down your variable expenses will not be enough. You would then need to work on trimming down your fixed expenses and figure out a way to supplement your income to balance your budget.

Chapter 3: Learn How to Save

Saving money might seem like a daunting task, especially for those of us who are frivolous spenders. You might look at your dwindling bank account statement at the end of the month, wishing you had saved enough money at least to get you through till your next payday, but wishes won't make the money in your account grow.

Saving money is a skill for sure, but one that you can learn very easily. As with most things in life, you just need determination and discipline to save money successfully. If you start feeling guilty just at the thought of saving money, or rather, the lack thereof, don't worry. We all have good intentions at the beginning while setting our budget or even resolving to save more this month, but one thing or the other always turns up, throwing all our grand plans in the trash. Maybe your car broke down, and the garage sent you an exorbitant bill, or your kid needs to get braces, or the thermostat in your house broke down, or there is mold growing in the kitchen. You have to make these payments, and so the concept of saving goes out the window. You keep assuring yourself that you'll save money once you get rid of all these pesky expenses, but that time never comes.

You'll always feel like a donkey chasing a carrot on a stick when it comes to saving money unless you learn some healthy money habits and determine what is more important for you—your current wants or your future needs. You need to make saving money a priority in your life and work hard towards realizing that priority.

Don't fret, though. Saving money might be a skill, but it is one you can easily learn. You will be surprised to learn that there are a lot of things you can do to save money; some are so simple, you won't believe you didn't think of them first yourself. All you need to do is tweak your spending habits a little, and you will breathe new life into your budget through practical money-saving measures.

Ways to Save Money

Say Goodbye to Debt

Debt cripples your journey towards financial independence. Paying off credit card debt seems particularly irksome, with its high interest rates. If you're in the habit of making minimum payments every month, you might feel like you are throwing vast amounts of money in the water without ever making a dent in the amount owing.

Debt robs you of your income, so you should make eradicating debt your very first priority. Adopt the debt snowball method, which is the fastest way you can get rid of your pesky debt.

The snowball method entails that you pay off your debt from the smallest amount to the largest amount. It sounds a bit overwhelming, but it can be done. It's more about changing your behavior and your mindset than changing numbers. You can Google the debt snowball method for further clarity. Once you are free from debt, you can finally work on saving money!

Cut Down on Groceries!

Wait a minute, you might say. How can I cut down on my groceries? I need to eat! You would be correct, but the whole point of this is to shop smart. Many people are astounded when they discover how much money they throw away at the grocery store every month. An average American family consisting of two parents and two kids spends around $929 at the grocery store every month. Yikes!

Curb your impulses at the grocery store and develop smart spending habits. Refrain from grabbing that extra bag of Oreos and chips and throwing all the shiny goodies they offer at the counter in your bag. You can also take advantage of store discounts and coupons to get some amount taken off your final bill. You can also research different stores in your area, as some stores price products higher than others. This also depends on your locality. If you live in a posh, upscale neighborhood, chances are the groceries in your local store will be priced a little higher than other lower-income neighborhoods.

Buying little things at the grocery store, a dollar here, a few cents there, might not seem like a lot, but the numbers add up, and these tiny things end up becoming major budget busters at the end of the month. If you must take your children grocery shopping, make it clear from the beginning that they are not allowed to add anything to the cart without your permission. Tell them strictly that you will only buy the things that you need and not an item more. The best thing to do would be to leave the kids at home altogether. However, if you have to bring them, make sure they follow the rules. You would do well to follow this rule as well.

You can also start by making meal plans each week, then buy your groceries according to that meal plan. Also, take a good look in your pantry to see what items you already have to avoid overbuying. Now that we are in the 21st century, you don't even have to go to the grocery store. Save time and money by ordering groceries online. This would also help you avoid the tempting sights and smells at the grocery store. You would end up sticking to your list and not splurging. A lot of grocery stores offer online discounts as well, so that is another incentive for grocery shopping online.

Cut off the Dead Weight (Subscriptions)

You might protest this one as well. You might say, "But I NEED my Netflix and Amazon Prime," and "The gym is the only thing keeping me fit and sane! I need it for my health." Yes, you do, but you don't need to spend a lot of money to do so.

You probably have multiple paid subscriptions to streaming services like Hulu, Netflix, and Spotify, etc., along with a fancy gym membership, those Instagram subscription boxes, and Amazon Prime. Sort through these and only keep the ones you regularly use, instead of just having them as a status symbol. Make sure you turn off the auto-renew option whenever you buy something. That way, if you have to go through the subscription process again, you would have to evaluate its worth every time you do so and confirm whether it is aligned with your new budget.

You can also opt for sharing your subscriptions with family and friends. Split the costs and reap the same rewards. As for gym memberships, the local YMCA or neighborhood gyms are equally as effective as Equinox. If you just need to work out, many online classes give you the same experience for very little money. You can also opt for discounted programs offered by several gyms that cut down on some of the value-added services but provide the same experience.

Get off the Brand Wagon

Name-brand products cost a lot more than generic products. One of the easiest ways to save money is switching to generic products. The only thing better about branded products is that they have better marketing. The products are the same. Generic brands of medicine, staple foods, cleaning supplies, etc., cost far less than their name-brand counterparts, and they work just the same. If you switch out the labels on the packaging, you won't even be able to tell the difference. This is about saving money, not showing off.

Sever Ties with Cable

Do people still watch cable TV these days? Cable prices are rising like crazy, averaging at about $107 per month. Why would you pay that much for TV? You don't even need it! If you're already paying for streaming services, you can opt for alternatives to cable and save a lot of money. There are network apps that you could use to get the same shows. Don't go overboard on the subscriptions, though—opt for the services you'd use and stick to them instead of paying for cable.

Go Automatic

Going automatic can help you save money without you even having to think about it. You can set up your bank account in a way that automatically transfers your funds from your current account to your savings account every month. If you don't trust banks and find this prospect terrifying, you can also set up your direct deposit to automatically transfer a portion of your paycheck into your savings account. You save money, you don't have to think about it, and you have an unyielding service that holds you accountable for your promise of saving.

Be Smart About Extra Income

The biggest problem with saving extra income is that we tend to think of extra income—as extra. We consider it a bonus, a free-for-all, an excuse to buy whatever we want because it is money we would not otherwise have. But that is a mistake!

If you ever get any additional income, which could be anything from a bonus at work, a tax refund, or inheriting money, you need to think about it as useful money—not as 'extra.' Put your money to good use. Don't go on a shopping spree or dump the money in your bank account. You should use that additional income to pay off debt or build up your emergency fund. If you get tax returns, you could always adjust the withholding on your paycheck, so you can bring more of your own money home every month instead of it going to the government.

Reduce Energy Costs

Most of us just accept whatever energy bills are sent to us from the electric or gas companies; we sigh and pay whatever amount we were charged, considering it the rule of the land. However, you do have a say in how much you pay. You can do this by making a few tweaks at home that can cut down on your energy costs dramatically. You can change a few simple things about your daily routine. For example, take shorter showers (you get just as clean in ten minutes as you would from a one-hour shower), fix all leaky pipes to avoid wasting water, wash your clothes in cold tap water to conserve heat, and install dimmer switches and LED light bulbs. Why would you use the old-fashioned, power-guzzling bulbs when LED lights shine just as bright and cost next to nothing?

Some people would advise buying energy-saving devices, but they cost an arm and a leg! The aim here is to save money, not spend it now so you might save some in the future. However, if you do manage to save up cash, you can buy these energy-saving devices so you can save even more in the future—but only if you have enough money to spend on them!

Stop Insta-Shopping

Scrolling through Instagram, you probably see many flashy ads that catch your attention. These products all seem so innovative and exciting, and everybody seems to be using them with the best results. Buying these products has never been easier. All you have to do is click a button. Your smartphone will enter your saved credit card details, and poof, the product is ordered and arrives on your doorstep within the week. Then the endorphin rush from the shopping wears off, and you're stuck with the bill, including the cost of the product, plus delivery charges!

While it might be super-enticing to buy the latest laxative tea, hair vitamins, or the newest fashion offerings from an 'Insta-store,' you will never be able to save money if you keep spending it on frivolous things. However, nobody expects you to give up shopping online altogether, and it's unfair to ask you not to buy nice things. What you can do is set a quota for yourself and budget for these online shopping forays. You can allow yourself to make one or two purchases a month, under a set dollar amount. That way, you won't feel deprived and still meet your budget.

Avoid Eating Out

Studies show that the average family spends about $3,500 on eating out every year. That's $300 per month! All that takeout and home deliveries when you don't feel like cooking don't seem like a lot, especially if you're ordering fast food, but those bills add up. A few brunches out with friends at your favorite restaurant each week costs a lot. And if you're in the habit of buying lunch during your lunch break instead of bringing a packed lunch from home, you're spending additional money on food when you already spent money buying groceries!

You'd be surprised to discover how much money you can save by packing a lunch and refraining from ordering food. Also, can you believe that you can buy a whole week's worth of groceries with the same amount of money that it would cost you to have two meals in a nice restaurant? Eat at home; it's healthier both for your body and for your bank account.

Don't Be Shy! Ask About Discounts

Many stores offer discounts and deals with certain terms and conditions. You just have to pluck up the nerve to ask. Many credit and debit cards offer discounts at specific stores if you use that card, and stores might have specific deals or sales that they don't advertise. You can also ask the proprietor about any package deals they can make to accommodate you and bargain where you can for a discount. Most people feel too shy and embarrassed to ask for these things because they are afraid of coming across as poor and pathetic. Don't be! It's your money! Why would you pay any more than what you have to? The shopkeeper won't judge you; chances are they do the same thing. It's called being smart and not throwing away your hard-earned cash.

So whenever you go out next, whether it's to the movies, a concert, or any game, you can ask if they have any special discounts. Most of the places where they charge entrance fees (like amusement parks) offer special discounts for seniors, students, small children, military, teachers, or AAA members. Even if they don't, talk to the manager nicely, and they might just do something for you! Just don't be pushy or entitled. Talking nicely to them might work; however, if it doesn't, be gracious and move on. You don't deserve a discount simply because you asked. It's still the proprietor's discretion, so don't be a jerk.

Take Advantage of Your Retirement Plan

Many employers offer retirement plans for their employees. In America, it's the 401(k), and almost every country has a variation of this. If you have one and you're not taking advantage of it, you're missing out on so much. Talk to your Human Resources department and set up an account. However, make sure you are debt-free and have a substantial rainy day fund before you start saving up for your retirement.

Try a Financial Fast

Challenge yourself. Go on a financial fast, where you do not purchase any non-essential items for a week. If it works, try going for a month. Freeze your credit card (quite literally if you don't want to be tempted to use it) or withdraw a certain amount of cash from the bank and resolve to spend only that much money during the set period. You can facilitate your financial fast by prepping your food at home, not going to the mall to avoid temptation, and not buying anything that is not essential to your survival.

Try these tips out. It's impossible not to save money if you do these right!

Chapter 4: How to Invest Your Money Smartly

Saving money is great, but as long as you're working a job, you can save up a good sum of money but never be really wealthy nor financially independent. The goal ultimately is to be financially free so that if one day you decide not to work, or when you retire, you have enough money in the bank to live comfortably and worry-free.

Being thrifty and frugal is great, but you shouldn't become miserly and scrimp on every bit of cash possible. Saving is not the only thing you need to get ahead financially. You need to earn, save, and invest. If you just focus on scrimping on money, depriving yourself of the things you need, it will only get you to a certain point and definitely could cause you to develop a poverty mentality.

What exactly is a poverty mentality? It's when a person becomes overly preoccupied with their lack of money, lamenting over all the things they don't have and can't get. They resign themselves to accepting that they are poor, that they don't deserve the best, and that this is their lot in life, so they best accept it. This is a self-limiting belief that causes people to make decisions based on a fear of loss or fear of failure.

Instead, you should have an abundance mentality. A person who has an abundance mentality or a prosperity mentality can make their decisions based on all the possible benefits. They are not reckless spenders. They appreciate the need to save money, but they are constantly thinking of ways to grow their income. They save and scrimp for a time, and then when they have money, they splurge and reward themselves as well. They believe they deserve the best life has to offer and work hard towards making it happen for themselves.

The best way to grow your income is through investments. The prospect of investing might seem scary to those who have never done it, but in this day and age, if you hope to acquire any form of wealth or financial freedom, you need to start investing.

Can I Invest?

When most people think about investing, they think about men with briefcases, wearing a suit, sitting in front of a computer looking at millions of dollars changing hands on a stock market app. That's not it. You don't have to be a Wall Street investor to start investing. You can start investing with even a few spare bucks. Compounding interest is your friend, and it will help grow your money.

You need to have good habits like regularly saving money. Once you have a tidy sum saved up, you can start investing. There's an app for everything in 2021, even for investing! All you have to do is get started.

Here are some places you can explore if you wish you start investing:

Investing in Lucrative Real Estate

There is no denying that investing any amount of money is a bit of a risk. However, when it comes to real estate, things change completely. Investing in real estate almost guarantees you significant profits and returns in the form of property appreciation, rent, and many other benefits that it holds. Of course, you can always live a life where you rely on paycheck after paycheck, but that is binding and can often be quite frustrating. Besides, relying solely on a salary will not bring you any closer to your goal of achieving financial freedom. Real estate, on the other hand, can certainly get that sorted for you.

Investing in real estate is both lucrative and highly in demand. There is something about owning your own real estate that leaves you burden-free, allowing you to sit back, relax and enjoy the countless benefits it offers. It is a true gateway to financial freedom for you and for those after you.

If you have inherited a property, your luck couldn't be any better. You can put any such property to good use, allowing you to generate an additional—and handsome—monthly income in the form of rent. However, there is one downside that you should know about; that is the cost of maintaining the property. Be sure to set aside some of the earnings to reinvest in the property and ensure its integrity and outlook. All in all, if you are not able to make matters work, you can always use the property yourself and take away the burden of paying rent. Furthermore, you will have something to pass on to your children as well, something not many people are able to do these days.

Owning property allows you to gain some tax advantages. If you were to claim depreciation of the property, you would end up paying less tax than you normally would.

Of course, it goes without saying that the real estate market is not entirely the most stable market in the world. It is still easy to see just how great the demand for houses, apartments, and commercial buildings is. Everyone wants one, and everyone needs one.

How to Start Investing in Real Estate

Obviously, the biggest question on everyone's mind is how to get started. Here is something for everyone to understand; you do not have to be super-rich to invest in real estate. You just need to play matters smartly, analyze the situation, and buy at the right time, at the right price.

For anyone looking to enter the world of real estate investments, there are many ways you can get started. Real estate is a great way to diversify your portfolio as an investor. The problem is that a majority have no idea how to begin, even if they have the money to invest. If you want to invest in real estate but have no idea where to begin, don't despair. To kick-start things, consider something called real estate crowdfunding.

What Is Real Estate Crowdfunding?

If you know anything about real estate or crowdfunding, using the words together may seem like an oxymoron. After all, real estate is from the old school of investing, while crowdfunding belongs to a relatively newer age of investors. Still, despite it being a novel concept, it is a good way to invest your money nonetheless.

Crowdfunding basically utilizes social media networks such as Facebook and Twitter to promote a new business and attract a wide range of single investors. You could be one of those investors and make a lot of money off these investments if you know what you're doing.

Explore Stock Options

Whenever the term "stock market" is used, people are quick to visualize all the massive boards, the charts fluctuating up and down, the red and green digits that keep on flashing, and the chaotic noise of the brokers yelling every now and then. Well, that is how a typical stock market works. The good thing, however, is that the internet has come to help. Now, you can invest your savings and capital in your favorite stocks and reap the benefits almost daily. Of course, it is slightly easier said than done. Besides, there is a substantial risk involved here, which is why many refrain from putting their hard-earned money into the stock market.

If you are someone who is afraid or has the same perception, don't be alarmed. While the risks exist, the rewards exist as well. Billionaires across the world invest a significant portion of their earnings into the stock market, which further goes to show just how lucrative the investment can be. If you do not have any idea about how stock markets work, you can always hire professionals that can help you manage your funds accordingly, allowing you to stop worrying about every minute that passes and enjoy the profits as they start flowing inwards. However, that option does cost a little more.

A better way to start would be to create an online investment account. The account will allow you to buy and sell shares of listed stocks and mutual funds as well. It is a great first step to take, allowing you to learn the finer details. A great way to start is by investing in low-cost index funds. These are essentially a type of mutual fund, in case you were wondering what these are.

Decide How to Invest in the Stock Market

There are quite a few options that you can explore with ease. We will be covering some of these options that should ideally be suited for beginners or first-time investors. These options won't necessarily work for everyone, but it is highly likely that beginners will find these more suited to their preferences and budget.

Selecting Stocks and Stock Funds

A hands-on investor would do well to select this option. Analyze what your personal needs are, and then select the right account accordingly. You can also compare different stock investments and choose the ones that best suit your needs.

Hire a Professional

Sometimes, selecting the right account, finding the right stock, and understanding why a given stock is right to buy can be quite cumbersome. However, there is always a way you can skip right past all that trouble and hire yourself an expert. To make things a little more interesting, you no longer have to rely on hiring a human expert either. Now, you have the option of using the services of something called a robo-advisor.

A robo-advisor is essentially a cleverly designed piece of computer software that runs 24/7 on your command. It manages your funds, invests in the right stocks, and pulls out when the profit hits a maximum point. It can also take care of the losses by setting limits, hence avoiding a complete washout of the account. Robo-advisors are great, effective, and do not cost a fortune either. Many leading companies offer these, which is why it is a good idea to contact the brokerage or firm that you are going to sign up with and see if they offer these services.

Investing in Your 401(k)

You can do as many beginners do—invest in your employer's 401(k) retirement plan. This is a good way for new stock investors to get started and learn all about the finest ways that have been tried and tested in order to scale up their savings. The returns are over the long term, and the contributions that you will need to make are significantly small in proportion.

The above does mean that you will need to take a hands-on approach, but then again, the efforts are worth the results. Once that is sorted, it is time to decide on what account you will choose to move forward with.

Choosing an Investment Account

It goes without saying that in order to invest in the stock market, you need a solid investment account, one that is trusted and reliable. The safest bet is to opt for a brokerage account, especially if you are trying to be a hands-on investor (being more involved). Alternatively, you could always open an account through a robo-advisor. As mentioned earlier, this is a good option if you are not too confident about going through the technicalities. Both of these accounts require very little investment to get started; however, it is still a good idea to check with the firm what their minimum requirement is for an initial deposit.

Opening a Brokerage Account

This is perhaps the quickest way to start buying stocks and possibly the cheapest as well. By having an online brokerage account, you can buy and sell stocks almost instantly and at the lowest price possible. You also gain access to a selection of other investment options that may serve you well. You will also have an option to open what is termed as an individual retirement account (IRA), but you will need a broker to help you with that.

Opening a Robo-Advisor Account

For anyone who is not looking forward to the technicalities and is hoping that they do not have to face anything that may overwhelm them, it is best to settle for a robo-advisor account.

When you open an account, the firm will ask you about your investment goals, what you wish to achieve, and what time period you have in mind. You are charged a nominal management fee, and pretty soon, your account is up and running.

It is pertinent to mention here that most robo-advisors charge around 0.25% of your total account balance. You still get to enjoy all the benefits, but you no longer have to worry about the decision-making process.

Try a High-Yielding Savings Account

Everybody knows about savings accounts, but they aren't a means of investment. Experts agree that putting your money into a savings account and allowing it to collect interest at a snail's pace is the worst way to invest your money, however risk-free.

Low risk always means low returns; the higher the risk, the higher the payoff. However, that doesn't mean all saving accounts are useless. You can always give high-yield savings accounts a try.

High-yield savings accounts are a type of savings account that offers Federal Deposit Insurance Corporation (FDIC) protection (in the US) and which have a much higher interest rate than your basic savings account. The logic behind it is that these accounts earn more money because you need to make a larger deposit initially to secure the account. Also, you have limited access to the account. Banks don't offer this account to just anyone; only customers who have other accounts with the bank can opt for this, and you would need to arrange transfers from other banks to deposit and withdraw funds from the online bank. Learning how to operate this account is a bit tedious, but the returns are worth it. Make sure you research before settling on an account as there are different kinds. Choose the one that helps you make the most money on your savings.

Try Peer-to-Peer Lending

Peer-to-peer lending is a novel way to make money, where borrowers are connected directly to investors through websites. These websites decide the terms for the transaction, including the rates, and facilitate the transactions as well. You can become a peer-to-peer lender.

Peer-to-peer lenders are individual investors who want to make higher returns on their cash savings rather than wait for interest to gather slowly in a savings account. Peer-to-peer borrowers are those people who don't want to take loans from banks and get investors at a better rate than what the bank has to offer.

Alternate Ways of Investment

You can also invest using the following methods:

- Use the Stash app: The Stash app is a personal financing app for beginners. You can download the app and explore it until you are comfortable using it. It is very easy to use and self-explanatory, and it is a great first step into the investment world.
- Certificate of deposit: Also known as a CD, this is a savings account that can hold a fixed amount of money for a predetermined period, with the bank paying interest on the money. You can redeem your CD whenever, and the bank pays you your original deposit and all the interest you made while the money was invested.
- Cookie jar approach: If you've never saved money in your life, try the cookie jar approach. Put away a small sum of money either in an actual cookie jar or any alternative that suits you. Try putting ten dollars in a cookie jar every week, just to get into the swing of saving. Increase that amount gradually, and you might find you have a substantial amount of money.

Now that you know all these ways to invest your money, you can get started on your journey towards financial independence.

Chapter 5: How to Achieve Financial Independence

Being financially independent means never having to worry about answering to someone else and depending on someone else for your survival. You would never have to worry about getting laid off from your job and could live comfortably based on the money you have, rather than always worrying about where to get more money from.

Still, even though being financially independent is a dream for many, only a few ever make it their goal. You need to have a better understanding of what financial independence means if you hope you achieve it. Luckily, that is where this book can help.

What Is Financial Independence?

Financial independence can mean different things to different people. However, the basic definition of the term means that you never have to rely on a job or anyone else for your finances, and you would still be able to uphold your standards and live a good lifestyle.

Being financially independent means that you have a fat savings account and multiple investments that supplement your income, which grants you your freedom, freedom to live the life you like on your terms.

How to Achieve Financial Independence?

Here are ways that you can work on acquiring financial independence of your own:

- Define what financial independence means for you: You need to understand what it means for you as a person to be financially independent. Picture yourself free from any financial restraints. What kind of life do you hope to live? When do you want to retire? Where do you want to live all your life? Do you want to work or want to achieve financial independence while still working because you enjoy your profession? You need to get a good idea about what financial independence means to you so you can set attainable goals to achieve it.

- Create measurable goals: Having goals that you can measure are much more attainable, and you can work towards them. For example, if it is your dream to retire at the age of 40 and move to the Bahamas, you can work towards that goal. You have assigned yourself a fixed timespan and a final destination. You can work on that goal until you achieve it.
- Make paying off debt a priority: Debt is like quicksand for your finances. It sucks up all your money and leaves you nothing to show for it. Pay off debt as quickly as you can, and only then can you save any money.
- Live below your means: Most people do the exact opposite of this. They have cobwebs sweeping through their bank account, yet they own all the latest designer clothes and flashy accessories to show off to other people on social media and in real life. By living below your means for a short time, you can save money until your investments pay off and you can afford to live according to your means.
- Create multiple income streams: By having multiple streams of income, you are not reliant on a single source of income for your financial health. You can supplement your income this way and put more money towards savings as well.

These are simple ways that you can follow to achieve financial independence.

Chapter 6: How to Build Wealth from Scratch

A lot of people dream of building wealth, but only those who follow through on that dream end up acquiring wealth. Anyone can build wealth if they have the right tools to do so.

What Is Wealth Building?

Wealth building means creating a stream of long-term income for yourself through various sources. This means having an income that goes beyond just your job. This includes any money earned through investments, savings, and any other income-generating assets you might possess. The wealth-building process relies entirely on financial planning and having a deep insight into your financial goals. Many people rely on wealth building to secure a strong financial future for themselves.

Why Is Wealth Building Important?

Anyone who desires financial peace of mind should work on building wealth. Living paycheck to paycheck is a stressful life, and any unforeseen expenditure throws our entire lives into havoc.

If you have wealth, you can define your standard of life. You would never have stress, even if you lost your job, because you would have a vast reserve of money to get you through that time. If you don't have wealth, losing your job can be terrifying and can run some very dire consequences. Everybody wants to be secure when they are old and retire; after all, nobody can work forever.

These days, hardly any employers offer sponsored pension plans. Some countries do offer government-backed retirement plans, but they are barely enough to fulfill even the most necessities.

How You Can Build Wealth Out of Nothing

Wealth building might seem scary and for rich people only, but that's simply not true. You can build wealth too. All you have to do is:

Believe in Yourself

You need to believe in yourself if you hope to accomplish anything in life. After all, why should anyone else believe in you if you don't believe in yourself? If you don't believe in yourself, you will never successfully build wealth. You need to have a positive outlook on your finances. Build yourself up, use positive affirmations to make yourself believe it will happen, and it will. Remember to think big and not be limited by a negative mindset. Think about the best version of yourself, preferably one with wealth. What would that entail? Once you have that idealized vision in your head, work on achieving it.

Have Better Spending Habits

Spending less money is much easier said than done, and saving your way to wealth may seem like a long and tedious process. You need to live below your means to build wealth out of nothing. A little sacrifice is necessary, but that doesn't mean you should deprive yourself of everything you like entirely.

You can, however, cut a few corners in the following areas:

Save on Housing

Don't live like the wealthy if you aren't wealthy! The nice house will come once you acquire wealth. Do not buy a larger home than what you strictly need. Also don't live in a very expensive area. Keep your housing costs in check, and you will save money.

A large home means more expenses with higher utility bills. You would need to spend a larger amount of money on heating costs, for example. Your home insurance will also cost more. Expensive neighborhoods come at their costs, such as having higher real estate taxes and higher-priced goods and services.

Also, when you want to repair or add things to your home, laborers will charge you according to the size of your home and the location of your neighborhood. Living in a high-priced locality will ensure high-priced bills.

Save Money on Transportation

Do not waste any money owning an expensive car, just for the sake of being able to say you have a nice ride. Expensive cars cost a lot to maintain and also consume a lot of fuel. Try opting for a small car instead—one that does not guzzle gallons of fuel and is easy and cost-effective to maintain.

Also, if you need a new car, don't lease it from the bank; save up cash and buy it.

One more thing you can do is buy a used car. People are apprehensive about buying used cars because shiny, brand-new cars are more appealing, and there is a misconception that used cars tend to be faulty anyway. That is not the case if you do your research and purchase a vehicle that has low mileage and is in good condition. That way, you avoid having to pay the hefty depreciation price that one has to pay once a new car is rolled off the car lot, and the car will be new for you anyway!

Keep your vehicle in good shape; have it detailed and regularly serviced. Make sure the oil is changed, and keep rotating the tires and replacing the air filters. Don't go to expensive chain auto shops and give your patronage to independent repair shops instead.

Spend Less on Food and Drinks

Limit dining out, as discussed before, and cut down on your grocery bills. You can save a lot of money keeping these few things in mind.

Create Wealth by Saving

The concept seems simple enough; save money, and over time you will have a substantial amount of money. However, saving alone isn't enough to amass wealth. You need to get creative with your savings and figure out ways that grow your income as well. This book has previously explained several ways you can save money. Utilize those methods to save, and then look for ways you can invest and grow that money.

Grow Your Income

Some things are easier said than done, but you can make more money. You just need to explore new avenues that will allow you to grow your income. You can make more money by doing the following:

- Negotiate a pay raise: Obviously, this is only applicable if you can do so. You would have a much better chance at negotiating a raise if you do your homework. Know your worth, do your research, figure out the market rate for your skillset, and find out what other companies are paying for your job. If you aren't getting enough money, point that out to your boss. If they refuse, ask what you can do to get a raise. It doesn't hurt to try, right?
- Get a higher paying job: If your current job pays you below the market value of your skills, switch! Why would you stay at a place that pays you less when you can get more?

- Increase your market value: Invest in yourself. Learn new skills or get certified in your profession. See how you can enhance your value to spruce up your résumé and get a higher-paying job.
- Try a side hustle: You can always try running a small business on the side to supplement your income. Start an online store or provide a service. You can also get a part-time job if you have the time.
- Freelance: There are so many freelancing jobs available online these days. Try platforms like Upwork or Fiverr, where clients are willing to pay for a myriad of services. You will be able to find something that suits your talents and skills.

You can also grow your income by:

- Eliminating debt: As mentioned before, you will never become wealthy with debt hanging over your head like an ax. When the ax falls, you could very well lose your head, or at least all your money. Pay off toxic debt first, then other debt. Once you're debt-free, you will finally be able to save.
- Invest! Refer to Chapter 4.

Chapter 7: How to Spend Money Wisely

As anyone who loves to shop will tell you, spending money is so easy! You could go to the mall and blow a thousand dollars in an hour if you had the chance. Have you ever been in a situation where you go to the mall, resolving not to buy anything other than what you need, and end up leaving with a ton of extra stuff, an empty wallet, and maxed out credit cards?

Some people naturally have poor impulse control and no idea how to curb their shopping habits. Others simply don't know how they can spend their money smartly, instead of just buying things and hoping for the best. If you keep spending money impulsively, you can say goodbye to the notion of saving anything or acquiring any kind of wealth.

Spending money smartly requires a shift in your mindset; you need to change your mentality to change your spending habits.

People experience financial struggles for different reasons. Some don't make enough money, while others spend way too much of the money they do make. Time Magazine estimates that nearly 73% of all Americans die in debt (Town, n.d.). Isn't that a depressing statistic?

If you want to avoid becoming a part of that statistic, maybe it's time you learned how to spend money wisely. This book is here to help.

Know Where Your Money Is!

Some people hate looking at their bank statements after making transactions because it's too painful to see the consequences of their reckless spending displayed tangibly in black and white. Most of us have been guilty of putting away an unpaid bill without opening it until the due date, and many of us still shove ATM receipts into our pockets or the trash, not wanting to look at how little money we have left in the bank.

Still, the whole sticking-your-head-in-the-sand approach never really works, does it? You have to be accountable for your spending. You need to keep track of your finances, so you know exactly where you're spending your money, down to the last cent. Use your budget, track your income, and once you know where your money is going, you can explore ways to make smarter choices about spending it!

Evaluate Purchases

Do you buy the first thing that catches your eye in a store? Have you ever seen something in a display window, felt attracted to it, and bought it on the spot, despite having no prior plans to make a purchase? That means you buy on impulse. Impulse purchases can wreck your bank balance. It's alright if you decide to impulsively buy a bar of chocolate at the supermarket, but impulsively making larger purchases will become a problem in the long run. So before you buy anything, evaluate its long-term benefits and drawbacks.

Is it going to last long? Will buying it put you in debt? Is it worth the money you're spending on it? Will you still feel good about this purchase in a week? Ask yourself these questions before buying something; then, the money would stay in your hands, and you would avoid impulsiveness and make smarter purchasing decisions.

Use Your Credit Card Smartly

Credit cards aren't bad—people just don't know how to use them. They are convenient and offer great deals on a lot of purchases. However, people often tend to treat credit cards like magic wands; they let you purchase things when you don't have the money to pay for them, but at the end of the month, when the bill comes, those wishes sour. So many people have maxed out credit cards because they treat it like a magic wand.

You should only use your credit card if you can fully pay it off at the end of the month. Making minimum payments adds a ton of interest to your bill. Plus, when you make a minimum payment, you're not making a dent in your bill. You're just paying the credit card company what it takes to keep you out of trouble for defaulting. Always pay the maximum, or at least pay as much as you can, to get rid of credit card debt as soon as possible. Utilize your cards for cash-back deals, redemption points, and discounts but only use 30% of the limit on your card each month, not more than that, and pay it off promptly.

Be Modest!

There are a lot of people who feel the need to maintain a certain lifestyle to portray a certain image of themselves to other people. Curating this image includes buying fancy cars, designer clothes, expensive accessories, and gadgets. Most people bankrupt themselves and go into immense amounts of credit card debt to try and keep this lavish image. They might buy new clothes just to post an outfit-of-the-day (#ootd) picture on Instagram, or go out to eat in fancy places just to post a picture of their plate with the fancy restaurant's location on display.

Not everybody is a Kardashian, and many certainly don't have Kardashian levels of money either. Trying to keep up is an extravagant and completely ridiculous pursuit. While it's okay to treat yourself once in a while and buy things that you like, don't get trapped in the vicious cycle of trying to live above your means just to impress people. People can see through the fake, and nobody likes a showoff. Save your money, live according to your means, and when you get financially independent, you will be able to buy nice things as well.

Figure Out Budget Draining Habits

Once you get into the habit of tracking your finances, you can use that information to discern which of your habits end up draining your budget. Are you spending way too much money ordering food or eating out, or buying too many clothes? There could be several financial drains that cause all your money to leak out of your account.

Once you decipher which of your habits are consuming massive portions of your money, ask yourself whether those habits are really necessary. What can you do to minimize your losses? The answer will come to you, and your finances will have a chance to heal.

Don't Commit to Any New Recurring Bills

These days, we are inundated with phone calls from bank marketing officers, selling us this loan and that. They make it out to seem as if you are special and that your income and your credit qualify you for these great loans for which you'd be an idiot not to utilize. Do not get deceived by these shiny offers.

Just because you qualify for a certain loan doesn't mean you should take it! To be honest, these bank officers will probably give you the loan even if you didn't meet their qualifications because they just want a way to get your money from you. Many people are naïve enough to think that the bank would never approve them for a credit card or a loan that they cannot afford. You'd be surprised at how many people get issued new credit cards with high credit limits when they already have many maxed out and defaulted cards lying in their wallets.

You see, the bank only knows your income, the one that you report yourself. They don't note any debt obligations or any other obligations, apart from those mentioned on your credit report, that could prevent you from paying your bills. Don't take on any more monthly payments than you have to. The bank doesn't know what's best for you; you do.

Value Savings Over Products

If you've ever seen an episode of TLC's *Extreme Cheapskates*, you would have seen a pretty extreme example of a person that derives immense pleasure from saving money and growing their wealth. These people will stop at nothing to save a cent; no personal sacrifice is too big, no humiliation great enough to stop them from hounding poor shopkeepers for deals and discounts. While these people might be certifiably insane, there is something to be said about their dedication to saving money.

Nobody is asking you to go to that extreme. But, some people are naturally very good at saving and feel content when they see their wealth growing. Other people spend their money the minute it touches their hand, believing that money is for spending now and that there is no point taking money to their grave.

Both are pretty extreme; moderation is always best in any circumstance. Money saved or invested will always help you in life, and if you value savings over products, you can turn those savings into products at any time in your life. Savings offer you long-term security, and they never lose their luster, unlike products that grow redundant over time.

Start Investing Early

It's never too soon to start investing. As an adult, if you find yourself wishing your parents had taught you about investing earlier, you're not alone. Wisely spending your money doesn't only mean avoiding buying unnecessary things. You also need to save money and invest it so that you can achieve the financial freedom you desire.

You are never too young or too old to invest. You're also never too poor; you can invest whatever little money you have saved in quality companies that grow in value over time. Figure out wise uses for your income (refer to Chapter 4), so you can gain financial independence.

You can adopt all of these practices to stop spending frivolously and start spending money wisely instead, and you will see the difference in your financial condition very soon.

Chapter 8: How to Be Financially Literate

The first step towards doing anything well is learning how to do it. Education is really important, in every aspect of life. Your finances are no different. You might have come across the term 'financial literacy' while you were looking up ways to save money or make more money. The term applies to how well you understand your finances and whether you make educated financial decisions every day.

The truth is, a lot of us lack when it comes to financial literacy. A CFSI survey conducted in 2020 shows that only 28% of all Americans are considered to be financially literate (Kunsman, 2019). You can choose to do better, and this book will help you do that.

What Is Basic Financial Literacy?

If you are financially literate, it means that you understand basic financial concepts. The benefit of understanding these financial concepts is that you would be able to make smarter financial decisions and autonomously make money choices.

Financial literacy can be defined as the ability to understand commonly dealt with financial issues such as saving money, debt management, investing, and paying bills. Being financially literate doesn't mean simply understanding financial jargon; it means being able to understand these terms to create financial stability in your life.

What Does Being Financially Literate Mean?

Being financially literate simply means you can perform some core functions such as budgeting and setting financial goals, and you understand the basics of loans (personal loans, debts, mortgages, etc.). You also know how to pay bills on time, save money, how to use credit cards, understand credit scores, and how to invest in different avenues.

You won't have financial literacy magically from the womb, and it's not something that is taught at most high schools. Unless finance is specifically your field of study, it's not something taught at university as well. Sometimes financial knowledge is passed down by your parents, but more often than not, you have to work at acquiring it yourself. We are fortunate to live in the internet era where we have a plethora of knowledge at our disposal. You can utilize that to learn about finance and become financially literate through self-study.

How You Can Be Financially Literate

Here is how you can gain financial literacy:

- Read books about finance: This might be a duh moment, but the best way to learn anything is to read about it in a book. Go to any public library and check out books on finance for free. Or you can always download ebooks about money management, finances, investing, etc. There is a wide range of topics available for your perusal. If you don't like to read, try audiobooks instead.
- Subscribe to financial newsletters: If you're not much of a book reader, you can read newsletters and magazines instead. Subscribe to financial newsletters that can get delivered straight to your email inbox. You can also get online magazine subscriptions such as the Financial Times and Forbes.
- Listen to finance podcasts: Podcasts are an entertaining way to learn. You get opinions from experts and learn about pretty interesting financial hacks and information. The best thing about podcasts is you can listen to them anywhere, in your car when you're driving, while you're doing chores, even while you're at work (if it doesn't impact your work, of course).
- Be on finance-related social media groups: You can find like-minded people sharing their experience and knowledge on these groups. It's a community of people, and you can find many who would be willing to help out a newcomer and give advice as well.
- Use financial management tools: Gaining financial literacy shouldn't be a chore. You can find a whole host of tools online that can help you gain more financial proficiency. These tools help you organize your finance and visualize your goals. You also end up learning a lot from them. Check out companies like Mint, Bloom, and Personal Capital. They can help you brush up on your financial literacy.
- Take a financial literacy course: You can get properly educated by professionals who teach comprehensive financial literacy courses. It's never too late to learn! Many colleges and schools offer external courses; you can look them up to see what suits you. If you don't have time to go to school, you can also get online workshops on platforms like Udemy, many for free and some that cost next to nothing.
- Break the consumer mentality: We are inundated with millions of ads on every platform every single day. The whole purpose of these ads is to entice you into parting with your hard-earned money. These days the capitalist consumer

mentality requires you to purchase more and more. Break that mentality. Being financially literate means being able to understand what is a wise purchase and what is an unnecessary impulse buy. Know the difference.

Hopefully, this crash course on financial literacy has inspired you to seek further knowledge. After all, nobody gets to be wealthy by being financially illiterate.

Chapter 9: How to Make Smart Financial Decisions

Now that you have learned how to make money, save money, and grow your money, it's time to learn how you can make smart financial decisions. We have to make financial decisions every day in our lives. These can range from figuring out whether you want to order dinner or eat at home to deciding whether to purchase a new home or not. Your financial decisions range from trivial to crucial, yet all of them must be made smartly. All of the financial decisions you make synergize over a lifetime to define your finances.

Making smart financial decisions will surely improve your quality of life. Here is how you can do that.

Create a Spending Plan and Stick to It

A spending plan is a budget. You learned how to make a budget in a previous chapter. You will never get ahead financially if you spend more than you earn. You could end up in financial ruin that way. You need to track your finances and stick to your budget. Sticking to your budget is the smartest financial decision you can ever make.

Get Out of Debt and Stay Out

Nothing sucks your finances out faster than debt. The first thing you need to do on the path to financial freedom is pay off your debt. Start from paying off the biggest and most expensive debt with the highest, most toxic interest rates (credit cards, we're looking at you). Once you get rid of that debt, work on paying off longer-term debts like your mortgage. Pay extra every month if you can afford it. This will trim years off the loan and save you thousands of dollars that you'd be otherwise paying as interest.

Set Savings Goals

Setting financial goals was discussed in detail in Chapter 1. Setting savings goals is the smartest way to gain some savings.

Start Saving Early

Compounding interest is your friend when you want to save. Even when rates are low, compounding interest allows someone who started saving early to earn a lot more on their savings as opposed to someone who started saving late. So start saving as soon as you can and put those savings in a high-yield savings account. It's never too late to save, but it's always better to get an early start.

Do Your Homework Before Making Big Financial Decisions

Some people do more research buying an iPhone than they do when buying a home. Don't be one of those people. Buying a home is one of the biggest financial decisions you will ever make in your life, so make sure that decision is smart. Do your research, find out the best property rates, and the best neighborhoods for your budget that serves your needs well. As a rule, if you need to buy anything worth more than a thousand dollars, you need to do your homework before buying it.

Avoid Impulse Buying

Don't make any financial decisions on the spot; there is simply no need for it. If you're ever pressured into making a quick financial decision, chances are, it's either a scam, or you're about to be suckered into a terrible deal. If something is legitimate, they will give you the time to consider and do your research before sealing the deal. Always remember that before making a major purchase.

Take Marriage Seriously

Researchers have discovered that married people earn higher incomes, have double the assets at retirement, and live on 25% less than what single people would need to earn to afford the same life. Statistics show that staying married is excellent for your finances. Getting divorced, on the other hand, could pretty much leave you bankrupt and destitute. If you don't have a prenuptial agreement, most countries split a divorced couple's assets 50/50, and you might be asked to pay compensation for any work your spouse has put in during your marriage. You will also be obliged to pay alimony and child support. So don't take getting married lightly; it's not only a lifelong commitment for your heart, but it also has a great impact on your financial health.

Feeling smarter already? Great! Implementing these financial decisions in your life will make you feel smarter still!

Conclusion

Now that we have covered all of the steps, you are finally equipped with all the tools that you could need on your quest for financial independence.

You know how to identify and set financial goals for yourself, which will act like your yellow brick road, with financial freedom being your Emerald City. Only you don't need a phony wizard to grant it to you; you will make it happen for yourself.

You have learned how to create a budget and stick to it. If you implement the 50/30/20 rule as explained, you should have no problem prioritizing and setting your budget according to your income. Hopefully, this will stop you from being broke at the end of the month, and you'll have money left in your account.

You also learned how to save money, a daunting task but deceptively simple once you get the hang of it. Gaining the discipline to follow through on all the tasks is hard, but if you have faith in yourself, there is no reason why you shouldn't be able to do so.

This book has taught you to invest your money smartly. Go over all of the options described in the book and figure out which method is the least scary for you to dip your toe into the investment waters. They might seem like they are shark-infested, but you have no cause to worry. You will reap the rewards in the end.

You have also learned the meaning of financial literacy, how to build wealth, and how to make smart financial decisions. Armed with all this knowledge, you can go forth on your quest, and hopefully, you will end up achieving your dream of financial independence. The world is your oyster, so go shuck it!

References

5 Smart Financial Decisions That Will Better Your Life. (n.d.). Monthly Finance News Magazine. https://www.finance-monthly.com/2019/08/5-smart-financial-decisions-that-will-better-your-life/

Bank of America. (2018). *Saving Money Tips - 8 Simple Ways to Save Money*. Better Money Habits. https://bettermoneyhabits.bankofamerica.com/en/saving-budgeting/ways-to-save-money

Berger, R. (2019, December 3). *12 Keys to Making Smart Financial Decisions (#7 is a Doozy)*. The Dough Roller. https://www.doughroller.net/personal-finance/12-keys-to-making-smart-financial-decisions/

Creating a Budget with a Personal Budget Spreadsheet. (2019). Better Money Habits; Bank of America. https://bettermoneyhabits.bankofamerica.com/en/saving-budgeting/creating-a-budget

Esajian, J. (2020, October 16). *What is Wealth Building & How to Get Started*. FortuneBuilders. https://www.fortunebuilders.com/wealth-building-assets/#:~:text=Wealth%20building%20is%20the%20process

Folger, J. (2020, February 27). *The 7 Best Places to Put Your Savings*. Investopedia. https://www.investopedia.com/financial-edge/0810/the-7-best-places-to-put-your-savings.aspx

Fontinelle, A. (2019). *Setting Financial Goals for Your Future*. Investopedia. https://www.investopedia.com/articles/personal-finance/100516/setting-financial-goals/

How To Be Financially Literate. (n.d.). Consumer Credit. https://www.consumercredit.com/debt-resources-tools/videos/informational-videos/how-to-be-financially-literate/

How to Build Wealth from Nothing in 8 Steps. (n.d.). Join Harvest by Acorn. https://www.joinharvest.com/how-to-build-wealth-from-nothing

How to save money: 11 Super simple money saving tips | Simply Savvy. (2017, May 8). Budget Direct Life Insurance. https://www.budgetdirect.com.au/blog/11-tips-to-save-money-in-tough-times.html

Town, P. (n.d.). *Spending Money Wisely: 7 Ways to Save More & Spend Less*. Rule One Investing. https://www.ruleoneinvesting.com/blog/financial-control/spending-money-wisely/

https://www.facebook.com/rule1investing. (2018b, December 21). *How to Invest Money: A Guide to Grow Your Wealth in 2019 | Rule #1...* Rule One Investing. https://www.ruleoneinvesting.com/blog/how-to-invest/how-to-invest-money/

https://www.facebook.com/thebalancecom. (2015). *10 Simple Ways to Manage Your Money Better*. The Balance. https://www.thebalance.com/ways-to-be-better-with-money-960664

https://www.facebook.com/thebalancecom. (2019a). *How to Become Financially Independent*. The Balance. https://www.thebalance.com/achieve-financial-independence-358175

https://www.facebook.com/thebalancecom. (2019b). *Your 6-Step Guide to Making a Personal Budget*. The Balance. https://www.thebalance.com/how-to-make-a-budget-1289587

Joy, D. (2015). *How To Set Financial Goals: 6 Simple Steps*. InCharge Debt Solutions. https://www.incharge.org/financial-literacy/budgeting-saving/how-to-set-financial-goals/

Karl, S. (2021, January 22). *What Is a High-Yield Savings Account?* Investopedia. https://www.investopedia.com/articles/pf/09/high-yield-savings-account.asp

Kunsman, T. (2019, November 11). *8 Simple Ways You Can Become Financially Literate on Your Own*. The Ladders. https://www.theladders.com/career-advice/8-simple-ways-you-can-become-financially-literate-on-your-own

Lake, R. (2020, October 5). *How to Achieve Financial Independence*. SmartAsset. https://smartasset.com/financial-advisor/financial-independence

Langager, C. (2019). *A Beginner's Guide to Stock Investing*. Investopedia. https://www.investopedia.com/articles/basics/06/invest1000.asp

McGurran, B., & O'Shea, A. (2021, March 17). *How to Start Investing: A Guide for Beginners*. NerdWallet. https://www.nerdwallet.com/article/investing/how-to-start-investing

O'Shea, A., & Davis, C. (2021, March 17). *How to Invest in Stocks: A Step-by-Step for Beginners*. NerdWallet. https://www.nerdwallet.com/article/investing/how-to-invest-in-stocks

O'Shea, B., & Schwahn, L. (2021, January 13). *Budgeting 101: How to Budget Money*. NerdWallet. https://www.nerdwallet.com/article/finance/how-to-budget

Ramsey Solutions. (2017, June 19). *How to Build Wealth at Any Age*. Daveramsey.com. https://www.daveramsey.com/blog/how-to-build-wealth

Ramsey, D. (2019). *How to Save Money: 20 Simple Tips*. Daveramsey.com. https://www.daveramsey.com/blog/the-secret-to-saving-money

Ramsey, D. (2021, March 1). *How to Set Financial Goals*. Daveramsey.com. https://www.daveramsey.com/blog/setting-financial-goals

Roberge, E. (2020, February 24). *Want To Make Better Financial Decisions? Start Here*. Forbes. https://www.forbes.com/sites/ericroberge/2020/02/24/want-to-make-better-financial-decisions-start-here/?sh=13ac5e5d3af9

Rose, J. (2019, September 26). *9 Ways To Build Wealth Fast (That Your Financial Advisor Might Not Tell You)*. Forbes. https://www.forbes.com/sites/jrose/2019/09/26/ways-to-build-wealth-fast-that-your-financial-advisor-wont-tell-you/?sh=424d22c67401

Schwahn, L. (2020, December 23). *How to Set New Money Goals*. NerdWallet. https://www.nerdwallet.com/article/finance/how-to-set-financial-goals

Sokunbi, B. (2021, March 23). *How to Spend Money Wisely: 5 Habits to Watch*. Clever Girl Finance. https://www.clevergirlfinance.com/blog/spend-money-wisely/

Taylor, P. (2011, March 18). *How to Spend Money Wisely (10 Things to Do)*. Part-Time Money®. https://ptmoney.com/how-to-spend-money-wisely/

The Smartest Things You Can Do for Your Finances. (n.d.). My Money Coach. https://www.mymoneycoach.ca/smartest_things_for_your_finances.html

Tom. (2020, May 14). *How To Build Wealth From Nothing*. Dividends Diversify. https://dividendsdiversify.com/how-to-build-wealth-from-nothing/